Jerusalem: City of Mankind

ירושלים

Jerusalem

القدس

CITY OF MANKIND

**Edited by
CORNELL CAPA**

Introduction
by
Teddy Kollek
with
J. Robert Moskin

HARRAP LONDON

EDITOR
Cornell Capa

ASSOCIATE EDITORS
Micha Bar-Am
Bhupendra Karia

SPECIAL CONSULTANT
Karl Katz

EDITORIAL ASSISTANTS
Edith Capa
Yvonne J. Kalmus
Enid S. Winslow

DESIGN
Arnold Skolnick

The International Fund for Concerned Photography, Inc., is a nonprofit educational organization which seeks to encourage and assist photographers of all ages and nationalities who are vitally concerned with their world and times. Among its aims is to promote and sponsor photography as the medium for revealing the human condition, commenting on contemporary events, and improving understanding among people.

First published in Great Britain 1974
by GEORGE G. HARRAP & CO. LTD
182-184 High Holborn, London WC1V 7AX

Text and Illustrations © *International Fund for Concerned Photography, Inc., and The Viking Press, Inc.* 1974
Introduction © *Teddy Kollek and J. Robert Moskin* 1974

ISBN 0 245 523987

Printed in the United States of America

Contents

Introduction

by Teddy Kollek
with
J. Robert Moskin

City of brotherhood and blood.
City of stone and flesh.
City of longing and hate.
Beloved city, remembered city, imagined city.
City of David, of Jesus, of Mohammed.

For endless millions through millennia, Jerusalem, crouched on the Judean hills, has marked the center of this world and the promise of one still better.

Those alive today have hacked the city apart, stitched it together with barbed wire, and then tried to heal it with the sacrifice of young lives. Its scars are livid, its stones silent, its faces tired.

Ahead for Jerusalem? Struggle certainly, but always the seed of hope. Leading its people is Teddy Kollek, the first Jewish mayor of the whole city of Jerusalem since the Romans destroyed it nineteen centuries ago.

As a young man, Kollek fled from Vienna to Palestine. Through the Hitler years and World War II he pulled Jews from the holocaust, and then smuggled guns out of New York so they could defend their Mediterranean beachhead. For a dozen years, he served the late David Ben-Gurion as director general of the Prime Minister's office in Jerusalem; endlessly energetic, Kollek actually ran the country day by day. After that, he was the crucial force in creating the Israel Museum above the Valley of the Cross, and in 1965 was elected mayor of the Israeli half of the then-divided city. Nineteen months later, suddenly, he was governing all of reunited Jerusalem.

The following pages are carved from the tapes of our three long conversations for this book. They are Teddy Kollek's very personal vision.

J.R.M.

E ach time I come back again to Jerusalem, drive around the bend in the rising road and see the golden city up on the hill, I have a special feeling. Over and over again. Hundreds of times. Whether I approach the city by day or by night, it is a beautiful thing.

There is a unique quality of life here, a sense of taking things in your stride: You will complete the task all right, even if it takes another day. There is a certain equanimity.

People here really care for this city. They have an intense feeling for their neighbor that does not exist in many cities today. I see examples of this personal caring every day, and it was especially discernible during the October 1973 war, when there was a tremendous amount of volunteering—at hospitals, at bakeries, at post offices. A lot of old people with cars drove children to school, drove the sick to hospitals, and picked up soldiers who came to town. In fact, we did not know what to do with all the volunteers. The people's greatest gripe was: Here we are and you are not making use of us.

The world must appreciate the depth of Jewish feeling for Jerusalem. Jews have fought more for this city than for anything else. In the 1967 war, many lives were lost because we would not use artillery to conquer the city. If you want to symbolize Jewish history in one word, the word would not be God. It would not be the Prophets. But if you say Jerusalem, it symbolizes the whole of Jew-

2

6

ish history through generations in one word. This has become part of everyone, even if he is not sentimental and not conscious of it. It is there. It is Jerusalem.

This meaning exists not only for Jews. The Crusaders came here; pilgrims through the centuries were willing to give up their lives for this city. You cannot separate Jerusalem from the feeling it has given people over thousands of years.

I share this feeling; to me, this is the most beautiful of all cities—a city that inspires more love from its people than does any other city in the world. It is an old city that has in our time become a modern metropolis.

The first time I saw Jerusalem, I was twenty-four. That was in 1935. I had come from Vienna to a kibbutz on the Sea of Galilee. After my third or fourth attack of typhus and typhoid, I was sent to a rest home outside Jerusalem. In a few days, I gathered a little strength and took a bus for half an hour and rode into Jerusalem for the first time. It was a little sleepy town, charming, with quaint corners and attractive people. Jews and Arabs mixed along the Jaffa Road. I walked the streets, walked in the Old City, and saw the synagogues and the Western Wall.

After 1948 and the birth of Israel, such a walk became impossible. Jerusalem, the divided city, was unbearable. To drive down so many streets and reach a sign that said, "Danger! Frontier Ahead! Stop!" was a traumatic experience every time. Cutting the city in two—blocking free access and the active interchange that goes on daily throughout a city and makes it what it is—was as immoral as dissecting any living body.

Much later, after I became Jerusalem's mayor in 1965, I hoped so much for the unification of the city that I canceled plans to remove the city hall from where it stood on the border between the city's two halves. I felt that this Municipality building opposite the Jordanian guns—from time to time being hit by gunfire on its southern side—represented the coming together of the city. When we started a city plan, we aimed for the year 2010—forty-five years in the future—and I said we should figure on the free flow of traffic in a single city. I knew the healing of the city would be a lengthy process, but I never doubted that it would happen. I did not anticipate that it would come suddenly and by violence—but it did come that way. Today, with the city united again after nearly twenty years, there may be more problems and frustrations, but there is a compensating greatness that did not exist before.

Probably no city in the world is more complex in its spiritual meaning, its heritage and history. Overlying the normal problems of a city this size—traffic and garbage and street signs in various languages—is a patina of religiousness and sacredness that gives Jerusalem its very special place in the world and makes it the center of so much concern.

The moment Jerusalem became one city it stopped being a Jewish city. It suddenly had a sizable population of Christians and Moslems. And ever since, we have been going through the process of absorbing this fact, not only intellectually but with all our being.

This has been difficult, of course, because religious Jews had prayed three times a day for two thousand years for the return of Jerusalem. It stood for independence and deciding your own fate and not being a minority. It meant everything that Israel means.

And yet we all realize that this city embraces both the past and the present. In that sense, Jerusalem can be portrayed as both a city of stones and a city of people. This book is a portfolio of beautiful pictures of those stones and those people.

There is something magical about the stones of Jerusalem. They are the past. The Moslems' Dome of the Rock enshrines a stone; the Wailing Wall of the Jews is built of massive stones; the Via Dolorosa of the Christians is an ancient way of stones. You can trace the long history of Jerusalem in its stones, from paleolithic times right through the gravestones of the wars of 1967 and 1973.

And the people. Their faces are so varied, so incredibly diverse. In 1948, there were 120,000 people on both sides of the divided city. Today there are 310,000 here. Soon there will be half a million. There are 220,000 Jews from more than a hundred countries, 70,000 of them of European or American origin and 150,000 coming from, or descendants of Jews from, the Arab and Moslem countries. There are now 75,000 Moslems and 15,000 Christians, among them Greek Orthodox, Armenians, Abyssinians, as well as some Arab Christians—altogether thirty-one different Christian denominations. It is this content from three religions that makes Jerusalem special.

One advantage we in Jerusalem have had in building a modern city and learning to live peacefully together is that we never had the ideal of the melting pot. The various groups of Christians, Jews, and Moslems have different languages, different alphabets, and different schools, and each assiduously protects its own different traditions. So they live together not in a melting pot but in a mosaic. It makes for less tension and for a pluralistic society in the best sense of the word.

Christian interest in the city is, of course, intense, even though the actual number of European Christians resident in Jerusalem may not be more than about two thousand monks and priests and others. It is a sad fact, I believe, that many Christians still have not become used to the idea that Jews are responsible for the governing of Jerusalem. At present, Christians leaders who are actively concerned with the city seem to feel that, although there are conflicts of theory, in practice Jerusalem is in good hands. During the Jordanian period, Christians were not allowed to acquire land to build churches and there was interference with their schools. Today, under Jewish administration, nobody interferes with the Christian holy places or with Christian pilgrimages or Christian schools. The Christians, like the Moslems, have responsibility for their own establishments and holy places.

Plainly, this is a complex, difficult, and endlessly fascinating city. The truth is, we have not learned how to run a modern city—anywhere. I am convinced that for a long time we will be struggling with the question of how to live in the cities. And Jerusalem has more varied problems than most.

For example, there is an extraordinarily high percentage of old people and children here, leaving a smaller than normal part of the population available to work. Many of the aged have come to Jerusalem because they have prayed all their lives to come. Among the young, we have ninety thousand in schools, from nursery level to the Hebrew University, an unusually large proportion of the city's population.

The biggest problem for the mayor of Jerusalem is the equalization of conditions among various groups—Jews and Jews and Arabs and Jews. Within the Jewish population, there are the secular and the pragmatic, the hard working and those who have other values for life: for many, Jerusalem's religious heritage is most important. There is even a small number who oppose the existence of the State of Israel because it was founded before the arrival of the Messiah.

The differences between the Jews who came from the Yemen and those from Germany, for example—that is, between the Oriental and Europeanized Jews—were not small, and we have not overcome them. In good part, solving this problem depends on the Europeans not insisting that they must turn every Moroccan Jew into the image of a Polish Jew. The major difference is that of values. The middle-class Europeans, over many generations, have acquired the Puritan Protestant work ethic: You have to work in order to achieve. And they think they express the only wisdom, that everybody has to fashion himself in their image. I would say this is a grave mistake when you are trying to build a city or a nation.

There is a story about a Mr. Cohen from Rochester, New York, who comes and meets a Jew from North Africa and asks him, why don't you work harder? And the North African Jew says, what would I do if I worked harder? The American says, you would make a little money and buy yourself a little shop and then, if you work still harder and treat your customers nicely, eventually you would have two shops and in the end you would have five; this is how I did it. What will I do then? asks the North African. And the American replies, you would save a little money. And what will I do with the money? Well, says the American, you would have leisure. And the North African shrugs and says, I have leisure already.

If we tone down the go-getting European drive to work and modify the "I have leisure already" attitude, we may do more for mutual understanding than by any other way.

One of our severe problems is that Jerusalem is a poor city, primarily for two reasons. First, it is a city of immigrants. Most of them come here without means and must be taken care of. The newest immigrants are the Russians; we have thousands of them in Jerusalem now. And even if they opposed the Soviet system, they lived in it and had grown accustomed to it. It is difficult for people who have lived all their lives in a regimented society suddenly to live in a free society. They are used to having housing allocated, for example, and have not had all the heartaches of selecting and competing for an apartment. In Israel they have to find jobs and refuse jobs. Even the way they send their children to school is different.

We have tried to help them by opening a bureau where they can talk with somebody and find out what to do. We have added a Russian section to the library. We provide special courses for their children in schools. Already, the Russian immigrants are contributing to the life of the city.

Secondly, Jerusalem is a poor city because it is not an industrial center; it has no port, and the nation's banking and business center is in Tel Aviv. We have some industry, but there isn't a single factory chimney here because we are very selective. And we would like to keep it that way. We have one factory that produces fine chemicals; it has twenty-four employees, twenty-three of whom are Ph.D.s. As long as it doesn't produce smells, I think this is ideally the type of factory we need, employing the people who are coming out of the university.

Since Jerusalem's economy is based mainly on gov-

ernment, education, and other activities which do not produce a great deal of taxable income, the city cannot pay for itself. Without support from the State of Israel, it would become again a deteriorating city.

On the other hand, this is a city with a tremendous amount of cultural activity. In addition to the Hebrew University, we have theaters, including the dramatic new Jerusalem Theater, a great deal of music, a half dozen museums: the Israel Museum, of course, and also the Islamic Museum, the Rockefeller Museum, a natural history museum, and private art galleries. We have many book shops. In our public library system, we have seventy thousand regular readers who use a million books a year (in Hebrew, Arabic, and many other languages), despite the fact that among the Arabs are many illiterates and among the Jews are many who would not read anything but a sacred book.

To me, the Israel Museum especially is not only a depository of great treasures, but a jewel of our city. It is one of our best pieces of architecture, sitting beautifully on the hill, beautifully lit, and with garden areas all around it. It has become a focal point for the city, where functions take place and people gather.

Most recently, we have created a retreat for the creative called Mishkenot Sha'ananim, near the King David Hotel. It had been an alms house built by Moses Montefiore over a hundred years ago and had become almost a ruin. We have turned it into nine elegant apartments with studios for musicians, painters, sculptors, writers, philosophers, and photographers. We are inviting people from all over the world to work and live and teach there for a while. And now they will come: Jorge Amado, Saul Bellow, Isaiah Berlin, Heinrich Böll, Henry Steele Commager, Louis Kahn, Elia Kazan, André Schwarz-Bart, Stephen Spender, Isaac Stern, and many others.

The retreat was opened last August with an evening concert. Pablo Casals was there, and he was so moved that he asked for his cello and went up and played. It was his last public concert.

We hope that this center will add to the cultural content of Jerusalem. When we restored the Khan, an ancient caravanserai, we turned it into a little chamber theater. We are now restoring the Tower of David and turning it into a museum of the city's history. A great museum, a great university give new content to an old city.

During the October 1973 war, all of these cultural centers were functioning. We tried to behave as normally as possible. The university continued its activities, although many of the professors and the Israeli students were not there, and some exams were postponed. We had concerts every noon at the Jerusalem Theater for the benefit of the soldiers' welfare fund. The people came and sat in the aisles; they sat everywhere. The Israel Museum was open. In 1967 we had put away all its treasures, but we didn't this time. Curators and typists filled in as guards and guides.

We are still creating more centers where diverse people can meet. We hope to turn the Jerusalem Theater into such a place. We built a walk along the city wall that has become a promenade of the town. We are making parks for the aged and a garden for the blind. We placed this garden where Jews and Arabs can meet. Before, it was a no man's land, where fighting was going on. Now, the blind will come there in peace.

We do a lot of things to try to bring Jews and Arabs

together. Perhaps the outstanding effort has been a summer day camp for young people; every day we had at least five thousand youngsters there. They were all mixed, Jews, Christians and Moslems. It would start early in the afternoon with sports and swimming and amusements; later, there were stage performances. We did it only for ten days because we did not have enough money to continue; ideally, there would be three or four such sessions a year.

Then, we have about two hundred Arab children in art and other classes at the Israel Museum. We are enlarging those facilities and want to build another Youth Wing at the Rockefeller Museum across town near the Old City.

For four years, we had mixed groups of Jewish and Arab high school students going to Europe and living together for almost six weeks. It was very effective. But we had to give it up because of the lack of money. Things like this could have a very significant effect in the long run.

We have several different school systems in the city, and Hebrew has been introduced in many of the Arabic schools, and Arabic in the Hebrew schools, as obligatory courses. My daughter, who is thirteen, started learning English two years ago and last year had to begin to learn Arabic, whether she liked it or not. She happens to like it.

Bringing Jews and Arabs together is valuable, but even more vital is to create equal opportunities for Arabs. We have built some Arab vocational training schools but need many more. Courses should be offered in electronics and television repairing and surveying and a hundred other things that will give them greater satisfaction as well as the chance for a better standard of living. If they can reach the same social and professional level as their Jewish neighbors, everything will become easier. And we also have to do more about the Arab housing shortage, for the Arab population is growing.

It is important that no one feels inferior. Despite the fact that we have 150,000 Jews who are refugees from Arab countries, and despite the fighting in Jerusalem itself in 1948 and 1967, we are doing everything we can to encourage Arab self-respect and self-confidence.

As a result, during the October war, we had not a single incident with the Arabs in Jerusalem. During those days, each one of us saw hundreds of Arabs; there was no tension, even though, obviously, they were not rooting for our victory. Normally, ten thousand Arabs come into the city daily as laborers and go home at night; during the war, the construction industry, in which many of them work, was virtually shut down because of the lack of transport, but they found ways to come in when there was work. We had a variety of decisions to make. There were two hundred Arab policemen in the city, all of whom were armed. Should we or should we not take their sidearms away? Of course, we didn't. They were policemen who had given their oath to carry out their jobs. There was no trouble.

During this war, the atmosphere in the city was much different from 1967. There was fighting then, and the tragedy of many deaths in the city itself was eased by the success we had; we got to the Wall; Jerusalem was reunited. This time, there were death notices from the fronts and many people in mourning and we had nothing to elate us and help us over the pain.

If the October war had any lasting effect on the city, it showed that the policy of fostering equality among all groups in Jerusalem has proven itself. Although Jews and Arabs had conflicting aims, we managed to continue neighborly relations. I do not want to say that all the Arabs are happy in a Jerusalem run by us. But starting from different points, both sides are anxious that the city shall be quiet, with no terrorism. No one can guarantee that a bomb will not be thrown, but you can walk about the city, day or night, in peace.

As I see it, the heart of the problem for the Arabs in Jerusalem is that they resent that they are not independent decision-makers with power over their own fate. We must find ways to assure them that the Arab character of the city will be preserved, giving the Arabs independence of decision within their own area, without again cutting the city in two. I believe I can say on behalf of all Jerusalem's inhabitants that, whatever their aspirations, they do not want to see the city divided again. From a practical point of view, a united city is unquestionably the only future we can look ahead to. And Jerusalem must continue to be the capital of Israel.

What will the Jerusalem of the future be like? It will certainly be bigger. The city is growing naturally, and also by immigration. We are constantly building new quarters, new housing. The new apartments on the French Hill are an abomination to some people who want the old Jerusalem preserved. But you cannot run a city on nostalgia, and those apartments are built of good Jerusalem stone and will in time become a very agreeable spot.

The most important fact about Jerusalem's future is that this will remain a mixed city. Of course, I am very much aware that we are running into dangers; I warn against them all the time. We can only do everything possible to prevent an explosion by curbing feelings of frustration. And I am talking not only of the mixture of Arab and Jew but also of the problems between Oriental and Europeanized Jews. To avoid tension in this mixed city, we have to anticipate and do things now that might better be done more slowly. This makes for tremendous pressures, but we cannot wait.

When I look toward the future, I see that the greatest danger is that meanings will gradually vanish. And this is true not only in Jerusalem. We are living in a secular age, and fewer and fewer people find spiritual meaning for their lives. People still search for it, but they don't find it.

Peace in this city cannot be taken for granted, but if people come here and the city is tranquil and attractive, they will stay to search for the meaning they seek, and maybe they will find it.

We in Jerusalem will do all we can to keep it a city of beauty and tolerance. This city has a mystique of its own. With it, perhaps we can develop a way of life in a mixed city that can be a model for others.

The remarkable collection of photographs in this book captures the life of Jerusalem as it is today and communicates it to the world. That makes this volume important. For if we can, in our one city, succeed in living peacefully together, perhaps, in that sense, the word of the Lord can go forth again from Zion.

Foreword
by Cornell Capa

"To capture the spirit" is the challenge and aim of all journalists, writers, sculptors, painters, and photographers. To capture the spirit of Jerusalem was a dream of mine which began shortly after the Arab-Israeli war of 1967. I happened to be an eyewitness to that war, and it made me aware of the important contribution photography could make toward an understanding of what makes this city so very special to its residents and to so many people all over the world. Subsequently I spoke of my dreams to Teddy Kollek, the mayor of Jerusalem, and the concept of the Triennale was born.

Two years ago, with the generous cooperation of the municipality of Jerusalem, Mr. Daniel Gelmond, Director of the Israel Museum, and Mrs. Elisheva Cohen, the Museum's chief curator, the International Fund for Concerned Photography began the elaborate preparations necessary to make the First Triennale of Photography possible. We began to search for photographers who could contribute something special to our understanding of Jerusalem: images that would bring us closer to the essence of this Holy City held so dear by the faithful of three major religions.

Subsequently, two major photographic exhibitions, "Jerusalem: City of Mankind" and "The Concerned Photographer 2," had their world premieres at the Triennale, which took place at Jerusalem's Israel Museum from September 1973 through January 1974. The first contained the work of twenty-one photographers—both Israeli and international—who have observed and recorded this unique city, each from his or her personal point of view. The show will tour the United States, starting at the Jewish Museum in New York City. This book is based on that show.

It is significant that Jerusalem was the venue of the First Triennale; I believe that it is the most logical place to make a statement on the human condition. Thousands of years ago, the message—in several versions—came from there in *words;* it seems fitting that a new message now emanate from there in *photographic images*—the universal language of the twentieth century.

The following photographers traveled to Jerusalem to seek their own answers: Robert Burroughs (American), Leonard Freed (American), Jill Freedman (American), Ernst Haas (Austrian), Charles Harbutt (American), Bhupendra Karia (Indian), Marvin Newman (American), Marc Riboud (French), Ted Spiegel (American), and Sherry Suris (American). From Israel came the work of Aliza Auerbach, Micha Bar-Am, Werner Braun, David Harris, Ron Havilio, Yoram Lehmann, David Rubinger, and Ricarda Schwerin.

All the photographs in this book were taken after 1967, except for those by the exceptional octogenarians Alfred Bernheim and Zvi Oron, the two pioneer photographers who are *part* of Jerusalem. Their work is not only historically important but transcends the boundaries of time. The Triennale paid them homage for their dedication to their city and for their important photographic contribution. For those of us who came later, Bernheim and Oron established the basis of Jerusalem's visual history to which we have added our own heartfelt observations.

My deep appreciation and thanks to all my colleagues who have contributed so vitally to this project, with an extra measure of gratitude and recognition to Micha Bar-Am, who acted as the Associate Director of the Triennale in Israel; to Bhupendra Karia, the Associate Director of the Triennale in the United States; and to our very special consultant Karl Katz, for his inspiration and insights.

Jerusalem: City of Mankind

David Rubinger

According to the Jewish legend there exists another Jerusalem—"Jerusalem of above"—of which the earthly Jerusalem is an exact replica.

The Jerusalem of
You and I;

The Jerusalem of
A Thousand Yesterdays and One Tomorrow;

The Jerusalem of
Golden Light and Black Shadows;

The Jerusalem of
The Golden Dome and The Begging Hand;

The Jerusalem of
Leaping Youth and White Beards;

The Jerusalem of
Love and Hate;

The Jerusalem of
War and Sabbath;

Jerusalem—where dissonance logically creates harmony.

3

Robert Burroughs

Jerusalem is such an old city, but it is growing young. It is an alive city, rich with culture and tradition, full of the confidence and frankness of youth that sometimes passes for arrogant rudeness. They don't appear to be tender people, these young ones, but I never saw an old person stand on the bus as long as there was a young one who could relinquish his seat.

4

Yoram
Lehmann

I have lived in Jerusalem for a great part of my life; photographing its people is a very personal and intense experience. I can no more describe my feelings about the subjects of these photographs than I could those toward a person whom I love. They are a part of me.

5

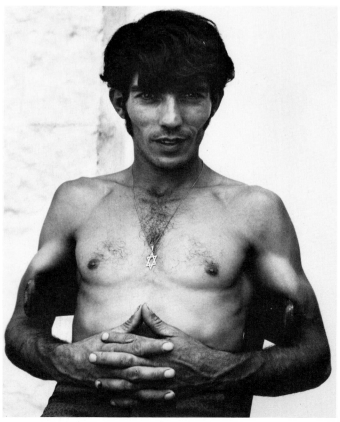

6

12

13

Zvi
Oron

Fifty-five years ago I decided to write the history of Palestine in pictures. Fortunately I came from a family of photographers and was trained in the profession rather early in life. When I fled from Czarist Russia to Germany in 1913, I found work on a Berlin newspaper. When World War I broke out I was in the United States covering the Jewish immigration.

After the Balfour Declaration, when Jewish battalions were being organized to fight for a Jewish home in Palestine, I joined the army. In my battalion were people like Itzhak Ben-Zvi (who later became the president of Israel), Levi Eshkol, and Shmuel Yavne'eli—all leaders and builders of Israel. We continually discussed the problems of the new state that was yet to be born. And I began recording the events of life in these early stages: the hardships; the happiness; the brutal murders; the Jewish intellectual pioneers alongside the Arab peasants; the rich, feudalistic Arab landowners who lived in luxury; and the British Mandate as it was—an imperialistic regime taking advantage of the whole situation.

As a former soldier in the British forces, I was able to become official photographer to the British High Commissioner and soon found the doors of the world press open to my reports. I eventually represented some of the most important American and European newspapers. As a reporter I won the trust of the Mandate rulers, the Jews, and the Arabs. The Jews accepted me because I told their truth; the British tolerated me because I represented influential newspapers; while my friendship with King Abdullah won me the courtesy of all Arab leaders.

To be able to record events as they are, one must be non-partisan and impartial. One must be a good observer. As a politician and a journalist it was a difficult decision for me to make, but I believed that a photographic history would ultimately be the most truthful. So from that day on I focused my camera and let it record what it saw.

14

15

16

17

18

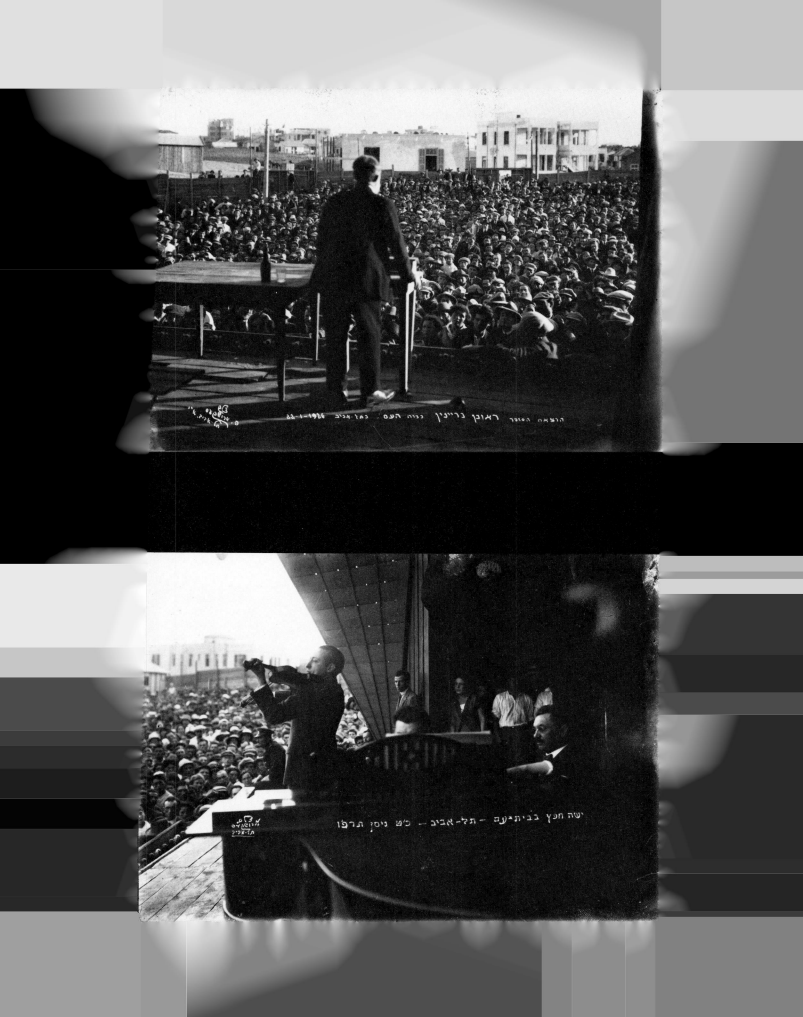

הוצאת הסופר ראובן בריינין · כבוד העם · תל-אביב · כ"ח·1·1·24

ישה חפץ בבית־העם · תל־אביב · כ'ט ניסן תרפ"ו

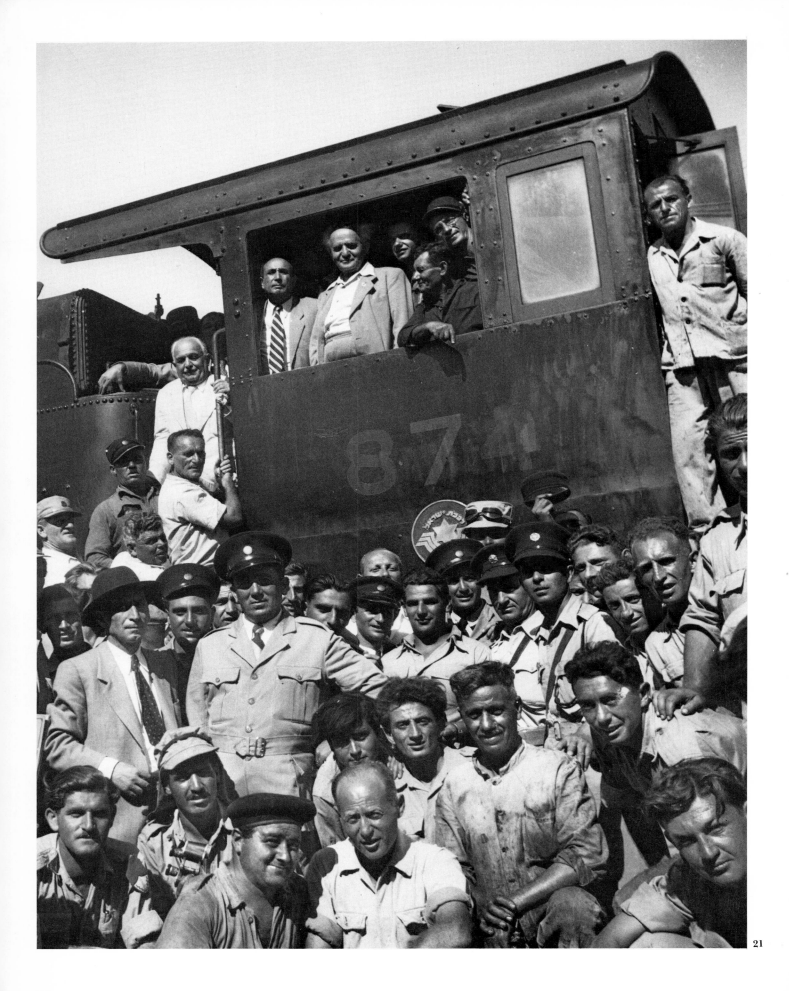

22

23

24

25

27

Cornell
Capa

Jerusalem is both the living symbol of man's highest aspirations and of his failure to attain them. It is the city that gave mankind a set of spiritual commandments: how to live in peace, how to live in harmony with each other. It is the city where the prophets lived, did not like what they saw, and predicted mankind's forthcoming, well-deserved doom.

Physically, Jerusalem is a very compact city. Within its ancient stone walls, everyday scenes are re-creations of familiar Bible illustrations; outside, it is a bustling, growing, twentieth-century city which is also Israel's capital.

The city is in a dramatic state of growth and transition. Jet travel and Jerusalem's unification have brought tourist-pilgrims in droves, giving many the chance to settle in the place of their spiritual longing. When everybody's dream has come true Jerusalem may lose its dreamlike quality, but I have not met a resident—be he native or one who just arrived "yesterday" —who was not apprehensive about such a possibility (or loss?).

Jerusalem is not a physical repository of spiritual values, a museum of dead artifacts, a curio shop for tourists. It is a *living city*—a queen whose loyal subjects of many races and religions jealously guard their love for her, each looking over his shoulder with suspicion for threatening manifestations of another's affections.

This is the oldest modern story ever told: Jerusalem, the City of Stones, is really the seat of man's deepest emotions.

26

27

THE CAPITAL
EPT IN MODERN LIVING
4 ROOMS
ROOMS
ROOMS
חדש במגורים מודרניים
4-3 חדרים
5 חדרים
6-4 חדרים
אדריכלים:
צ'רני את קפלן-ישראל
ג.ב.ר. ושות' קנדה
ARCHITECTS:
CHARNEY & KAPLAN ISRAEL
B.R. ASSOCIATES CANADA

Micha
Bar-Am

To me, Jerusalem is a city of endless contradictions—of cloistered quarters living side by side, being part of each other yet worlds apart. Individuals and communities complement each other and become part of that great, fascinating entity called Jerusalem.

Moslems, Jews, and Christians of all shades and denominations pray to the same *one* God—each in his own way and in his own language, crossing one another's paths on the way to the Dome of the Rock, the Holy Sepulcher, or the Western Wall. They meet wearing prayer shawls or miniskirts, bearing old wooden crosses on their shoulders or trays of fragrant fresh bread on their heads, or carrying ceremonial palm branches or baskets full of fruit.

Once, while traveling in what seemed to be a Godforsaken part of Africa, a man asked me where I came from. "Jerusalem," I answered. He looked at me, smiled unbelievingly, and said, "But Jerusalem is up in heaven...." Maybe he was right. It could be either way since, after all, she is both earthly and divine.

32

33

34

36

37

38

41

39

40

Ricarda
Schwerin

Again and again I am drawn to the diverse religious manifestations in Jerusalem: the casual intimacy with God at the Western Wall, the loftiness of the mosques, the rigid yet colorful Byzantine ceremonies of the Christian communities behind which all the loneliness of the young monks and nuns seems to be hidden. Perhaps it is the very contrast, and even contradiction, between myself and this exotic, esoteric world that has created this strange love affair between me and the soul of this city.

The different communities go on living in their old ways regardless of what happens around them. What unites them all is the need to live in Jerusalem, each according to his own light. What all of them lack is better knowledge and understanding of each other.

41

42

44

Sherry
Suris

To reach Jerusalem: a dream of peoples through the centuries. In the eyes and faces of Christian pilgrims and newly arrived Jewish immigrants from Russia, I saw the realization of the dream. It was a spiritual transformation. Jerusalem!!

The Christians, in prayer, glowed softly with a calm, a peace—a personal peace of believers communicating with God in the Holy City itself. These moments were undisturbed. They allowed for distraction neither from the people around them nor from the world outside. Everything beyond the communion of the Two (Man with his God) seemed, in fact, non-existent.

The eyes of the Russians reflected the weariness, the strain, the struggles of the past. But I sensed a strength as well, a strength rooted in the dream: "To reach Jerusalem before I die."

46

47

48

49

51

52

53

Bhupendra
Karia

As a strong September sun beat down on men and stones, I
walked the winding road from Silwan village to the Dung Gate
wondering about the special Middle Eastern secret of self-
preservation. Mercifully, one does not have to wander too far
in this quest. The olive trees, the rolling hills, the marble and
the mosaic of Jerusalem—all surviving centuries of extreme
exposure—have insights to impart.

The walled city has a distinct quality. The clanking, hawk-
ing, incessant mercantile activity in the bazaars veils the grace-
ful pace of the back streets where arches of brilliant light and
velvety shadows, like some huge walk-through diamonds,
glisten with softly reverberating *salam alaikum*s. Narrow, me-
andering, mazelike streets seemingly come to an end only to
usher one into the tranquil, spacious, tree-studded compound
of the El Aqsa mosque whose marble shadows, like the wisdom
of the ancients, envelop one in awe. The bright Bedouin blan-
kets of the marketplace exist side by side with the elegant inlays
of the Dome of the Rock, which sits serenely like a poet wrapped
in an embroidered shawl contemplating the Mount of Olives.
The persistent, hard-bargaining merchants of the fluorescent-
light world are transformed into gracious hosts by evening, just
as the day's relentless heat gives way to cool, caressing breezes.

Everywhere I went, people welcomed me with warmth. In
friendship they politely expressed their natural apprehension
about pictures: "We hope photographs can express the truth."

Fortunately, the language of pictures, like the language of
friendship, is very straightforward and uncomplicated. As a
vehicle of expression, the spoken language is like a motorcar:
it travels smoothly along paved roads, meets a linguistic barrier,
and turns around. The photograph is like a helicopter: it takes
over where language leaves off, transcends linguistic limits, and
lands in the heart of the matter.

I am convinced that photographs made with an honest
understanding of, and an abiding respect for, the total social
landscape of a people can form vital bridges of communication.
In time, people visiting each other across such bridges would
inevitably discover their own truth together.

59

Werner Braun

Here am I, wed to my camera by a marriage of love, and before my eyes the dazzling kaleidoscope of Jerusalem unfolds. My mind is preoccupied with the events of the city: the Friday procession winding along the Via Dolorosa, attended by Christians from all over the world; the Moslems shooting their vintage guns every nightfall during Ramadan; the Greeks, Latins, Armenians, Syrians, and Copts all taking their turn for prayer at the Holy Sepulcher and sometimes quarreling over this precious little bit of *terra sancta;* the endless happenings at the Western Wall where the *shofar* is blown at the end of Yom Kippur, the *lulav* is brandished at Succoth, *matzah* picnics are held during Passover, and endless Bar Mitzvahs are celebrated on Tuesdays and Thursdays. My curious camera eye wants to record the ultramodern Denmark School in Katamon; the re-creation of a modernized, still old-fashioned, Jewish Quarter in the Old City; the sun shining through sculptures at the Billy Rose Garden of the Israel Museum; police girls meeting in small clusters to gossip instead of unraveling the eternal traffic jams. I am spellbound by it all.

In the Passover Haggadah, it is written: ". . . And next year in Jerusalem." This has been obsolete for me since 1946; that's when we settled here. I have been conscripted as a soldier for the defense of Jerusalem three times since then, making this very unique city grow extremely close to my heart. What we settled in was a sleeply, provincial, quietly scholarly town. The unification of new Jerusalem with the Old City in 1967 after the Six-Day War actually was a fertilization process. And what changes have occurred in its wake! I might not like everything that is going on, but I am part of it. And the Jews, the Moslems, the various Christian faiths, the atheists, the fanatics, and the tolerant ones will all have to live together in this strange melting pot. The Sleeping Beauty period is over.

Jerusalem is living history.

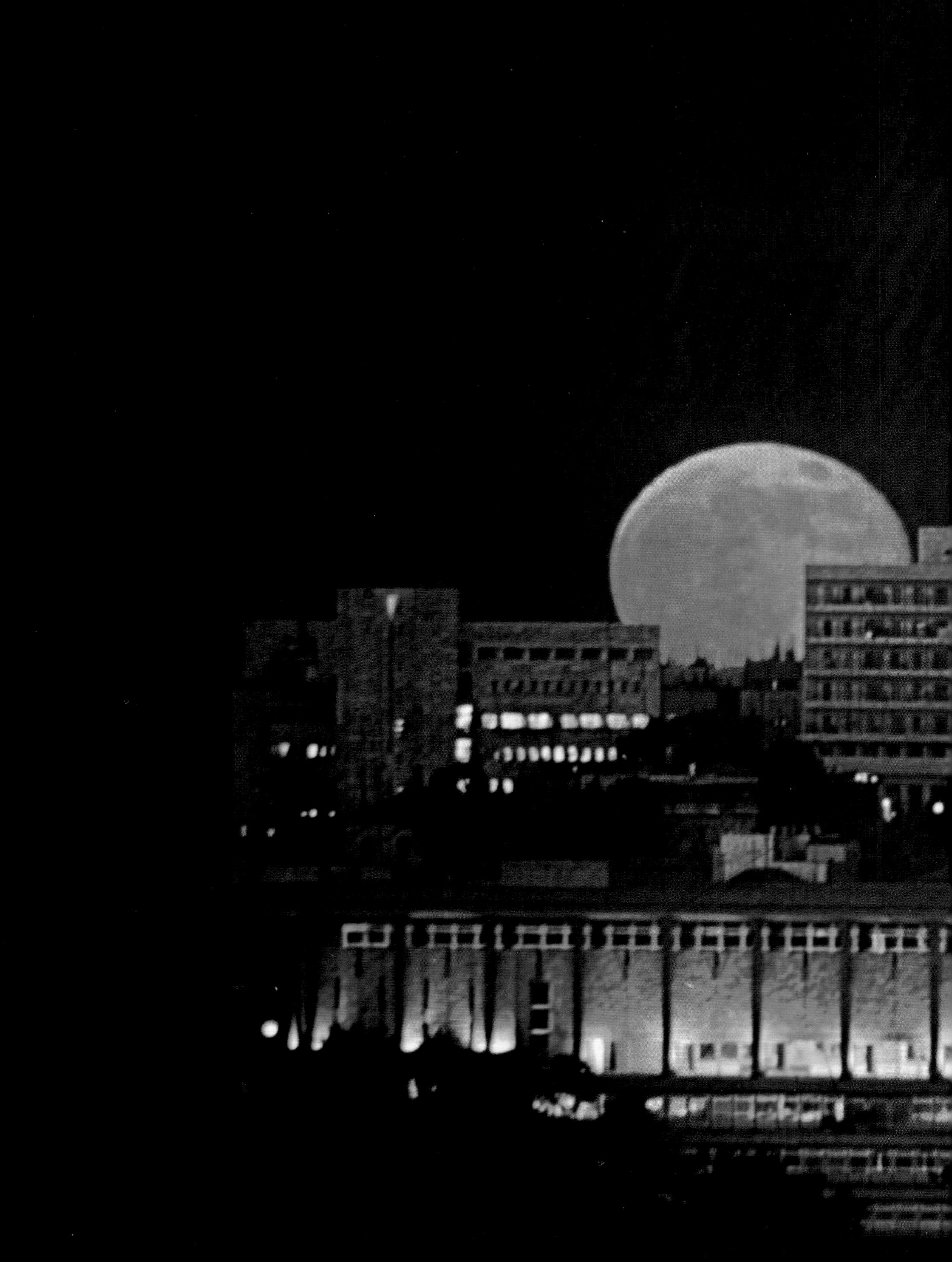

Ernst
Haas

Jerushalom . . . Jerusalam . . . Jerusalem . . .
How similar—how different.
Are you capital
Or the center of the three ways to only one God?

This mutuality became the point of division.
One did not fight for material stones
But for the radiance of their meaning.

You were made by change and you will grow through change.
Jerusalem, you were never property,
Only possession,
As you were always lost by the one who tried to keep you.

You are a paradox,
As one can't prove you
Without proving oneself.

Jerusalem, you who mean peace,
Show us the way to your deepest destination.

Jerusalem, you who mean peace,
Help us
So we can fulfill the meaning of your name.

Charles Harbutt

Faith, hope, and the anger of centuries-old religious feuds mark the Christian Holy Week celebrations in Jerusalem. Copts stone Copts on the rooftops of Good Friday churches and Armenians punch Greeks (who punch back) inside Holy Sepulcher on Holy Saturday. There is a competitive foot race among sects; during the last century, a treaty had to be negotiated to try to organize it all.

Yet through the melee marches a seemingly endless procession of simple people: Greek, Italian, and Lebanese women (black dresses, babushkas, and cotton stockings); an occasional wandering Russian mystic pilgrim; a brown-robed Franciscan from Ohio; a French Little Sister of Charles de Foucauld fresh from her life in some rancid city slum; the ubiquitous red-cheeked and sandaled Dutch missionary; and an Englishman in a fit of fainting—whether from the food or fervor is hard to determine.

The wonder of it all to a cynical, post-consiliar, ex-Catholic like myself is that people are there at all. God is dead, according to *Time* magazine. Why do they bother? Why are there so few rich? And educated? Where are the swingers? The bikers and dopers? And not one Greek jet-setter?

Then from a church, following the once-a-year-like-clockwork Holy Fire "miracle," a woman emerges cradling a dubious flame. She will take it to some damp village church or stone farmhouse crèche and brag for a lifetime of her pilgrimage. But she won't kill anyone or drive them insane or rob in the trillion-dollar bracket. And I had to wonder. It may not be that there is something in the specific goals of the pilgrims (or their brothers at the Wall and the Rock); but there is something here in Jerusalem's stones that makes one wonder and question and search. Perhaps that's more than enough for a Holy City to do.

Ted Spiegel

Rejoice ye with Jerusalem
And be glad with her,
All ye that love her;
Rejoice for joy with her,
All ye that mourn for her;
That ye may suck, and be satisfied
With the breasts of her consolations;
That ye may drink deeply with delight
Of the abundance of her glory.
—ISAIAH 66:10–11

The prophet Isaiah speaks of a joyous Jerusalem and of a troubled one. Glory and consolation are found in the same phrase, just as they are found on the same pathway in Jerusalem today.

Just east of the Judean hills which Jerusalem crowns, the great descent begins into the cleft of the Dead Sea; along its arid shore, geologists can measure strong gravitational forces. Approaching Jerusalem's focal point, the Dome-enclosed pinnacle of Mount Moriah, the humanist senses strong mystical forces. Abraham was drawn here to offer his only begotten son, Isaac, in sacrifice; in the dramatic encounter with an Angel of God, the patriarch entered into a covenant that has profoundly affected mankind. David fought for domain over the young Jebusite town and bought its summit—then being used as a threshing floor; it became the site of David's Altar and Solomon's Temple of Jerusalem. Artisans came to create handsome craftwork here, destroyers were urged to lay waste here; prophets proclaimed here; and Christ lived—and died—here. From the rock within the Dome, the steed Al-Burak bore Mohammed into the presence of the Almighty.

In all its diversity, mankind flows through the gates of Jerusalem. Go with Everyman along its intense way and you will see him living in the peace of Jerusalem, a very human peace. Had you asked him to speak of his life here, he would not have said the same things that his acts say.

So let the camera be a witness to actuality.

Marc
Riboud

I walked and walked in Jerusalem, and I looked.

I saw stones worn by the sun and the wind—beautiful stones worn by centuries of conquerors and pilgrims. I saw shrines and graves blending with the landscape because they had always belonged to it. I saw faces as worn as the stones—beautiful faces of many different races, revealing a faith whatsoever the creed and revealing a dignity whatever the humiliation. I understood how these faces, these stones—whether Jewish, Moslem, or Christian—make the soul of Jerusalem, and how deeply that soul is rooted there.

But I saw also the sudden superimposition of another ultra-modern civilization not rooted there, the bulldozer and the crane becoming as common as the pilgrim, a new skyline foreign to this sky and this land. Speed and efficiency are the new rites. The rhythm of centuries, Jerusalem's own pace, is being accelerated to the tempo of an assembly line.

This frantic race to anchor—with steel and concrete—new roots on a new soil has to brave the dignity of a large group of people. As on many faces, I saw humiliated pride on the faces of two Palestinian women. A bulldozer smashed through their small orchard; the next day, the whole family was expelled from the old stone house which had been theirs for generations. Offered a meager compensation, they lifted their heads and refused the alms. I understood how dignity is much dearer than an improved standard of living for the people of this land, and how Jerusalem belongs to this pride as much as it belongs to the pride of a courageous and victorious army.

But the builders of new Jerusalem know it better than others. What is built on humiliation seldom lasts long; the most unexpected can be expected from a humiliated people.

90

91

93

Ron
Havilio

Time and mysticism are all present in Jerusalem. These ancient walls of stone, these decayed windows, are marked by the footsteps of those who are no longer with us.

My photographs do not represent actions. They must be viewed on a more contemplative basis. The apparent distance and coldness, the static aspect, the simplicity and nothingness, lead the viewer to a visual meditation.

But explanations can only limit the image and its eloquence.

Jill
Freedman

People touch more in Jerusalem than they do in the West. Children are always carrying or hitting each other; men hold hands, so do women. Crowds of them push and squeeze and bump together, rushing through the streets as they rush through their lives.

The street is theater, and it's home. They eat on it, love, drink, shout, gossip, sweat, and curse on it. They litter extravagantly, sharing their garbage as readily as their humanity. And even when they are still the street moves, carried along by the momentum of thousands of years.

The new city feels more alive. There is more curiosity and impatience there, more diversity. The Old City is an ancient supermarket, where things are brought in rather than made. Jerusalem, the golden city of shopkeepers, where everyone is selling something and everyone else is buying. Moses. Jesus. Mohammed. Gold. Dresses. Eternal shoppers, doing time in the Holy City. Working the same hustles since the Bible was a short story.

And all the while, children forever race down the same old streets, recycled past old people cuddling babies who have their faces. And the Eternal City, running its human race through time, never changes, just grows older.

98

99

102

103

Leonard
Freed

I was brought to this quarter of Jerusalem called Bet Yisrael by a black-bearded, gentle young man in his twenties. Having traveled the world, he had now come to live in Jerusalem with his young family in a modern but Orthodox suburban community. "You know," he said to me, "like most Jews I lived in a Christian world. In my thoughts and actions I could just as well have been a Christian. At last I have come back to being and living what I have always been—a Jew. Do you remember the other day? It was after the evening service and we were in the Yeshiva. The Hassidim formed a circle in the center of the synagogue and each locked his hand in the hand of another. Even the Misnogdim joined in. Without musical instruments, we made music; without dance steps, we danced. The joy, the warmth, the electricity flowed from hand through body to hand. It was like we were holding hands with God."

Why had my friend brought me to this lackluster courtyard?

Near one small window an old man worked by the light of day, thus saving the expense of electricity; for a pious man, the light was more than sufficient to meet his needs. Old as he was he could still see, and his hand—a magnificent hand that had become a finely tuned instrument after a lifetime in service—could still letter in the words for a new Torah. When he wrote, he used the finest parchment and quill, the most expensive materials, contrasting to the shabbiness of his surroundings. What he wrote he did exactly as he had been taught as a youth; nothing—not a word, not a period—was to be or could be changed. Though he wrote from memory, he knew that it all would be scrutinized down to the last dot by the most competent authorities. While he wrote his face shone with an inner light of one in communication with God. For what was he but an obedient servant of God, writing down the words of God?

107

108

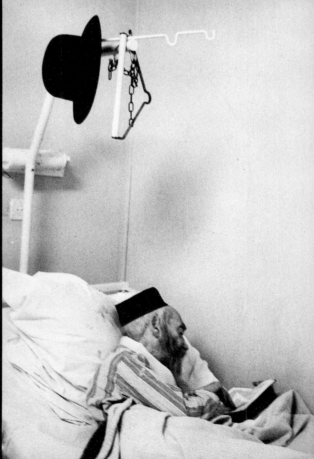

109

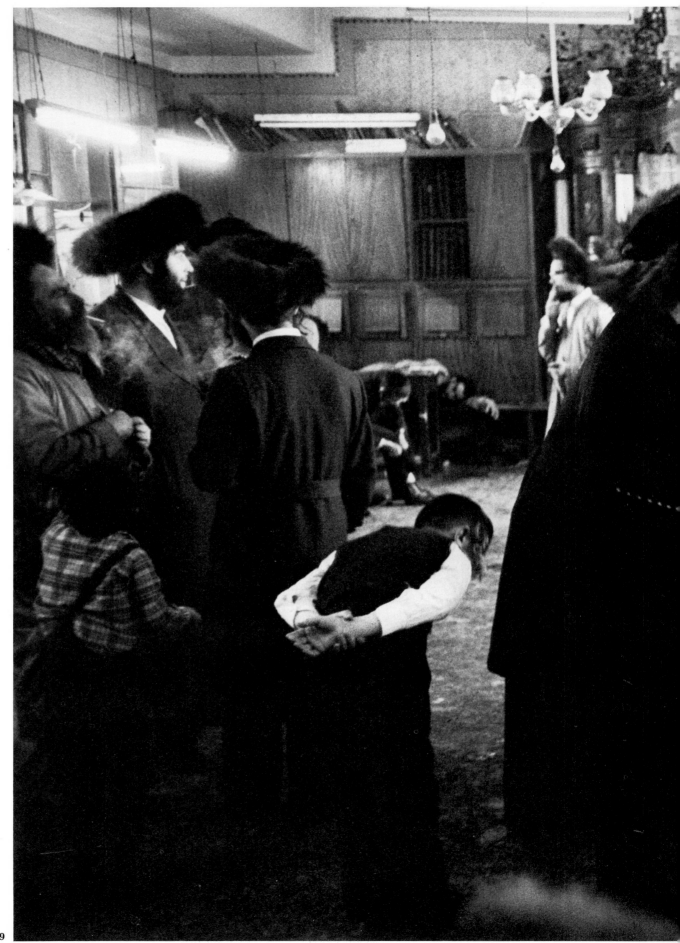

David
Harris

The Hebrew University is part of that confrontation between the old and the modern that pervades all alike in the city of Jerusalem. The young student reaches out for twentieth-century knowledge in much the same atmosphere breathed by David and Solomon. He studies the ancient Jewish philosophers, and his Talmud is the rectangular concrete forms of a new campus. Underlying it all are the inexorable realities of the Middle East which force him, as in the description in the Book of Nehemiah, to build his future with one hand on the sword.

113

114

115

Aliza Auerbach

Jerusalem . . . When I mention the name, I see the white Jerusalem of summer when the brightness is blinding and the nearly cruel light is thrown at you from every stone. I see Jerusalem in the rays of twilight—neither orange nor pink nor purple—which embrace the surrounding mountains and caress its houses of stone.

There is the Jerusalem of *Shabbat*. It's so quiet everywhere; even the traffic lights rest. Then slowly people start to be seen: old couples, fathers holding their children's hands, mothers pushing baby carriages, people going to and from the synagogues. It's the only place in the world with such calmness and so much tranquility.

The Jerusalem of my student days is not the Jerusalem of today. It was more like a little village then; everyone knew everyone. You could celebrate a different holiday every day of the year here if you wished.

It is hard to describe Jerusalem in words. One has got to feel it. Jerusalem is the source. It's the heart and the spirit, the soul and the oversoul.

118

119

121

Alfred Bernheim

As I understand the photographer's job, he is a painter, only not with brush and paint. I have been drawing and painting all my life. I am a portrait artist, even if my task is to take pictures of a tree, a building, or a single stone. I approach photography as a painter, not as a reporter. I'm always trying to bring out the essence of the subject.

Buber I did many times; I knew him in Berlin and then I met him again in Jerusalem. We spoke German because he hadn't learned Hebrew. When people asked if he had learned enough Hebrew to make himself understood, the answer was that he hadn't yet learned enough Hebrew to make himself *difficult* to understand.

When I photographed Rabbi Meltzer, his son brought me to their house. We went into a large room full of old furniture and books. My wife, who used to assist me, wasn't allowed to enter the room; no women were permitted there. I set up my big camera and three or four flood lamps, and then I asked the Rabbi to sit down. Although I said this and that to him, he never said a word. Finally, when I was finished, I thanked him but still he didn't respond. He didn't know he had been photographed because the sound of the shutter was so quiet.

S. Y. Agnon was probably my hardest subject. In front of my camera, he just froze. In the end, I played a trick on him: I connected a very long trigger-cable to the camera; then I stood in a corner of the room, clicking the shutter without approaching the camera. Agnon never noticed.

Henrietta Szold was the easiest to do; one photo did it. She liked the picture very much, but the Hadassah women rejected it. They said it made her look too old—she was then seventy-five. I wanted to order a taxi for her because it was raining, but no, Mrs. Szold—with her umbrella—preferred to walk. In those days, people walked much more than they do today.

120

List of Illustrations

ALL PHOTOGRAPHS EXCEPT THOSE OTHERWISE DATED WERE TAKEN IN 1972